Here Comes a Storm

By

Jemima Love

This book is dedicated to El Shaddai

"Big momma said it is a shame
to go outside in all this rain.
We should stay at home and pray
than be at school on such a day."
"My little Natasha you may be right.
This wind is giving me a fright.
Let us all kneel down and pray,
while the LORD has his way."

Bless the Lord O my soul.
Great is God our Lord.
Light covers you as a garment.
You are worthy to be adored.
You stretched forth the heavens as a curtain,
As the morning glories sing.

You make the clouds your chariots.

You walk upon the wind's wings.

You laid the foundations of the Earth
that it should not be moved.
Waters once covered the mountains
then fled at your rebuke.
The waters fled at your command
up high and down low.

You have set its bounds here and there
for places it cannot go.

You send springs of water into the valley
which run among the hill.
It gives drink to the animals
and the donkey gets its fill.

Your trees O Lord are full of sap
Lebanon's cedars you have planted.
There the birds make their nest
There desires you have granted.

You make lightening for the rain.

You bring forth wind from your treasuries.

You tread upon the waves of the sea.
The Earth shows forth your glories.

Your whirlwind goes forth with fury.
Yet you still answer out of the storm.
Those that are kept in your presence
are always safe from harm.

Most gracious God we lift you up,
And give you all the praise.
Your works are unsearchable.
No man can know your ways.
Great God we hear the wind subsiding.
You're bringing your peace again.
Now we can see your sun a shining.
In Jesus' name we pray
Amen.

Bible Study

(All verses are copied from the King James Version of the Holy Bible)

Psalm 104

[1]Bless the LORD, O my soul. O LORD my God, thou art very great; thou art clothed with honour and majesty.

[2]Who coverest thyself with light as with a garment: who stretchest out the heavens like a curtain:

[3]Who layeth the beams of his chambers in the waters: who maketh the clouds his chariot: who walketh upon the wings of the wind:

[4]Who maketh his angels spirits; his ministers a flaming fire:

[5]Who laid the foundations of the earth, that it should not be removed for ever.

[6]Thou coveredst it with the deep as with a garment: the waters stood above the mountains.

[7]At thy rebuke they fled; at the voice of thy thunder they hasted away.

[8]They go up by the mountains; they go down by the valleys unto the place which thou hast founded for them.

[9]Thou hast set a bound that they may not pass over; that they turn not again to cover the earth.

[10]He sendeth the springs into the valleys, which run among the hills.

[11]They give drink to every beast of the field: the wild asses quench their thirst.

[12]By them shall the fowls of the heaven have their habitation, which sing among the branches.

[13]He watereth the hills from his chambers: the earth is satisfied with the fruit of thy works.

[14]He causeth the grass to grow for the cattle, and herb for the service of man: that he may bring forth food out of the earth;

[15]And wine that maketh glad the heart of man, and oil to make his face to shine, and bread which strengtheneth man's heart.

[16]The trees of the LORD are full of sap; the cedars of Lebanon, which he hath planted;
[17]Where the birds make their nests: as for the stork, the fir trees are her house.

Psalm 135
[7]He causeth the vapours to ascend from the ends of the earth; he maketh lightnings for the rain; he bringeth the wind out of his treasuries.

Jeremiah 10
[13]When he uttereth his voice, there is a multitude of waters in the heavens, and he causeth the vapours to ascend from the ends of the earth; he maketh lightnings with rain, and bringeth forth the wind out of his treasures.

Job 9
[8]Which alone spreadeth out the heavens, and treadeth upon the waves of the sea

Jeremiah 30[23]Behold, the whirlwind of the LORD goeth forth with fury, a continuing whirlwind: it shall fall with pain upon the head of the wicked.